I0763608

Hindsight

Erin Geary

"There are years that ask questions
and years that answer."
Zora Neale Hurston

TABLE OF CONTENTS

VOLCANO

I was seven years old when NASA knocked Pluto from the Solar System: my first loss. Lucy Rodriguez held a memorial service at recess and all the second-graders sickled around, somber. We kneeled on the blacktop as Lucy lined-up eight kickballs and one tennis ball, labeling each with sidewalk chalk: Mercury, Venus, Earth, Mars, Jupiter, Saturn, Uranus, Neptune, Pluto. Lucy was a tiny girl who grew up to be my high school's shortest graduating senior. I think she felt some sort of camaraderie with the dwarf planet. She delivered a dramatic eulogy about its long and wonderful life, mimicking the rhythm and body language of a mourning adult. Halfway through, she borrowed Joey Matteo's Poland Spring bottle and splashed her face with water. The droplets glistened on her cheeks, catching the sun. The entire event was performative in a way that's unique to the playtime of children.

A teacher, Mrs. Reid, took note of the growing crowd. Her voice boomed behind us. "You're being terrible friends to Pluto," she said, causing us to freeze.

"I love Pluto!" Lucy attested, pushing her glasses up on her nose. "That's why I'm doing this!"

"Pluto wasn't big enough to be considered a planet! He was pretending and he got caught. Those astronomers told his secret to the world. Now, he's mortified."

We were stunned. Lucy's head dropped. Mrs. Reid grabbed the tennis ball and tossed it over the fence, freeing it.

"Let Pluto figure it out. Nobody knows who they are—not even the planets."

I was put into her class the next year.

Mrs. Reid loved volcanoes. She read us six or seven books about Mount St. Helens, which was her favorite, because her mom and daughter were both named Helen; Helen ran in her family. Mount St. Helens was dangerous. In 1980, it erupted violently and demolished hundreds of homes. After realizing its power, it had been quieter, as if it had learned its lesson. Mrs. Reid always emphasized its appearance, how it poked the sky, snow-capped, sure-of-itself. It was beautiful. She loved that it was a paradox. Mrs. Reid loved anything contradictory.

She was old. I didn't fully notice until much later, but there were clues. Her hair was silver and every time she climbed the stairs, she'd fold in half, out-of-breath. Despite her age and wisdom, she would never talk down to us. By eight, we could already identify the infamous *Kids-Say-The-Darndest-Things* smirk whenever it appeared on adults' faces. Our earnest, often misinformed, beliefs were constantly being reduced to a joke and we knew it. (This is the reason children stop asking questions; It's not because they know everything, it's because they don't.) Mrs. Reid didn't have a condescending bone in her body. In fact, *we* were *her* role models. Her speech unfolded like ours: boundless and imaginative. She was a vanguard of language, spinning it however she pleased.

One day during science, she taught us the difference between solid and liquid matter through an experiment in which she dropped a heavy thermos on the floor. It landed with a thud and didn't move. "See! This thermos is a solid." Then, she lifted it back up, unscrewed the lid, and poured its contents—24 oz. of coffee—down in the very same spot. The coffee ran feverishly in all directions. We lifted our sneakers, giggling, thrilled, as it meandered underneath us. "Solids don't change shape, but liquids do. When the coffee was in the thermos, it was the shape of a thermos. When the coffee was on the floor, it tried to take the shape of the room. If I had more coffee, I could fill the entire school like a giant bathtub!" Instead of reaching for the paper towels right away, she left the skinny rivers of coffee there until lunch. I was always jealous of the way she didn't mind mess.

I recall this experiment fondly, though I never associate it with the states of matter. Maybe I'm just not a science-person. In my head, this was a metaphor for how Mrs. Reid viewed language: like liquid. Sure, words could be defined by their usual solid, the dictionary, but they could also be bent, stretched, shaved-down, and reinvented. They would fit wherever they were poured. It was this leniency that made Mrs. Reid the best storyteller I have ever known.

When she was about to launch into a story, she'd rest a

single finger on her lips and wait. I'd belly with excitement. Mrs. Reid's stories were always borderline-fiction. They'd begin with a "normal" event—her walking her dog or eating dinner—and they'd end under-the-sea, in space, in Hogwarts, Neverland, Whoville, or Oz. Her character would begin to fly. Her dog would turn into a robot. The dinner would disappear. I couldn't always tell where the real part ended and where the made-up part began. Mrs. Reid claimed it didn't matter. "*The* story doesn't have to be *my* story," she'd say; it was her favorite mantra.

I had a secret. Every time Mrs. Reid took us to the school library, I would get really overwhelmed. I'd retreat into a corner, behind a tall shelf, and sit criss-cross on the floor, isolating myself from my friends. If I stayed hyper-focused on the spines of the books, all peeled and yellow from grade-school hands, then I'd be able to make it through the trip. If not, I'd feel winded and nauseous, an invisible pain, everywhere and nowhere at once. This didn't start happening until I graduated from picture-books and realized stories could be sad and often were. Mrs. Reid noticed right away—early September. Each week, she'd come to me with a book in hand, like a delivery or a gift. First, it was *The Miraculous Journey of Edward Tulane*, then *Because of Winn-Dixie, Bridge to Terebithia, Tuck Everlasting, Holes*, *Matilda*, *Harriet The Spy*. Curating our two-person book club became her unofficial side-job, one she admitted she enjoyed. She didn't outright ask what upset me so much about the library; she just seemed to know instinctively. "Read up to chapter five," she'd say. "We'll read chapter six together on Monday." This meant chapter six was The Sad Part. There's always a chapter six—even in books meant for kids—because without chapter sixes, nobody would appreciate chapter sevens or chapter eights. I didn't understand this yet.

Once I got good at it, reading felt like chewing gum; it became more about habit than flavor. I could sit for hours loving on a book until it bent loose and floppy in my hands. I started noticing everything, like the way my Mom pronounced the word 'idea.' If I listened closely, I could tell she was saying "idear," babying it on the pillow of her tongue, tucking it in, kissing its bald head. It was a speech pattern I could've adopted, but didn't. I'd say "ideeea," like it was a child faking sleep, a troublemaker. The more I read, the more I started believing these strange, abstract observations were useful. Nowadays, I wake up early, mining through books with a highlighter in hand, collecting. I use the word 'collect' here, because of its numerous definitions: 'to gather together,' 'to accumulate for storage,' 'to regain control over oneself, typically after a shock.' When horses *collect*, that means they bring their hind legs forward, increasing their balance as they move. Language buoys me.

Mrs. Reid's daughter Helen came to visit in February. She wore a red flannel and had a tiny gold hoop hanging from her septum. If she were a volcano, she'd be one moments before eruption. Mrs. Reid introduced her as an 'artist.' She squatted down so we were eye-level and started telling wild stories about her life doing special-effects makeup and prosthetics for sci-fi movies in Hollywood. As she was talking I looked at her tattoos. She had a whole sleeve of them. I wanted to ask her what each one meant, but I was too shy. I thought tattoos were cool, but I'd always have nightmares about getting ones I didn't end up wanting.

"Hollywood!" Joey Matteo cried after hearing her spiel. "That's where celebrities live!"

Helen laughed. "Mrs. Reid used to live in California too," she told us, gesturing toward our teacher. "She grew up there! My grandma used to bring her and her siblings to Venice Beach and they'd run around on the pier all day long."

Mrs. Reid rubbed her eyes and began rummaging through our classroom library. She read us two new Mount St. Helens stories after recess.

My best friends at the time were Julia and Kimmy McFadden: twin girls with fiery red hair that rode horses every weekend. On the bus, the three of us spent the entire last month of school daring each other to get sixth-graders to sign our yearbooks. There was this one girl, Chelsea, whose hot pink bra strap perpetually seemed to be sliding down her arm. We thought she looked like Britney Spears, if Britney Spears were 11. She sat in the back, against the emergency-exit, with her knees jutting into the aisle so she could oversee the rest of us. Chelsea was the kind of girl who wrote, "Have a Kick Ass Summer," instead of "Have of Great Summer," in people's yearbooks. She was goddess-like to us.

We were way too shy to speak to her, so Julia bought this fancy set of gel-pens and wrote "Chelsea" in each of our books, in curly script, the way we assumed sixth-graders wrote. We took turns pretending to be her, sometimes having full conversations amongst the three of us where, for instance, Julia would act as Chelsea, Kimmy would be Chelsea's best friend Jada, and I'd be Chelsea's fifth-grade sister Tess, who was younger than them, but older than us, still someone who chewed Big Red gum instead of Juicy Fruit, who called it 'hanging out' instead of 'having a playdate.' All three of those girls frequently wore ripped jeans, so if one of us could smuggle home safety-scissors from the classroom, we'd fray the inside-pockets of our pants, trying to initiate ourselves into their world while still being able to tuck back into our own.

As our third grade days dwindled, Julia admitted she had a crush on Joey Matteo and suddenly wanted to sit four seats back from our usual spot on the bus in case he dropped a

Pokemon card, so she could pick it up and hand it back to him. One weekend, she and Kimmy begged their dad to take us to the mall. He trailed behind while we smelled candles at The Body Shop and bought matching keychains at Claire's. On our way out, I realized why they'd wanted to come. Near the front entrance was a water fountain that acted as a meeting place for a knot of local teenagers. We walked past Chelsea and her older friends. She laughed as one boy crudely reached into the water and pulled out a handful of other people's coins. Kimmy waved to the crowd, linking arms with me—comfortable, as if we went to the mall all the time, as if we weren't kids.

Growing up meant playing the part through-and-through, even in private. "Remember how we used to have those underwater handstand contests?" Julia asked on one hot day as we were reading magazines by the pool—her choice. "That's so *embarrassing* to think about."

In class, I started writing a mystery story about a little girl who wakes up smaller each day. She gets so small that everyone has to start using a magnifying glass to find her.

"Is this story about you?" Mrs. Reid asked after reading it, raising an eyebrow.

I shrugged, vulnerable. I didn't want to be decoded so easily, but my fiction has always been thinly-veiled memoir.

"I've been teaching third-grade for 35 years. I've heard

this story before," she claimed, waving my book back-and-forth like a flag, emblematic of little girls throughout history, so naive. For some reason, what she said made me feel worse. Not only was I babyish and behind, but I wasn't even special in being these things.

"Don't be ashamed," she said, reading the feeling right off my face. "We all lose our childhood. We have to lose the weight in order to grow."

I paused to think about it, then said, "It's like getting haircuts."

"Haircuts?"

"If you cut the dead-ends off, your hair grows out stronger."

It suddenly seemed like a stupid comment and, for a second, I wished with all my might that I could reign it back in, until she said, "Exactly. Brilliant." Then, "I'm not afraid of getting older anymore. *Older* is what you make of it."

"I bet you're not afraid of anything."

"I'm no different than you."

"Well, you're a teacher."

"Exactly," she said. "So are you."

Mrs. Reid was a poem. I am her heirloom.

On the last day of school, we all gathered on the rug and Mrs. Reid handed us marble composition notebooks. She told us to carry them around all summer. Holding up a blue Moleskine, she said, "I have one too. Journaling is how I translate this world from its language to mine."

Mrs. Reid was old. As we were packing up the classroom one last time, she told us she was retiring, moving to California to be closer to Helen. I wasn't sure if she meant her mom or daughter, or both, or the volcano, but I knew she'd be happy there. I hugged her before I left for the bus, feeling her heartbeat through her shirt, a fragile sensation I didn't like and still don't. "It feels like I have a hole in my stomach," I said.

"Fill the hole with something else, something more permanent," she explained, unlatching herself from me, pointing to the composition book laying on my desk. "Our story is only over when you say it is."

EXPIRATION DATES

The Weaver family lived briefly in the blue ranch down the street from me when I was quite young. I loitered around their house a lot because I was close in age with the daughter, Karla, who was an only child. Karla was a tomboyish soccer player, known to wrangle up the neighborhood kids for a game. We had a lot of fun together.

I noticed things at the Weaver house that I never noticed at mine. Josie Weaver wept when she was tired, and when her husband, Phil, came home from work, he'd put the back of his hand on her forehead as if he were checking for a fever. At the time, I thought this was shorthand for *I love you, I got you,* but now I realize it was only ritual, quite arbitrary, like waving hello or goodbye. Their relationship had a strong architecture. Every Friday, Phil would bring Josie flowers from one of those kiosks in Grand Central. She'd put them in a glass vase, removing the wilted ones from the week before, then give the pink paper-wrapping to Karla and I. We'd fold it, accordion-style, and fan each other, or crease it into an airplane and send it fluttering out the window. I was caught up in the romance of it all, the bone-structure of Josie and Phil's couple. I never contemplated how silly it was on its skin: the quick replacement of flowers, the forging of something new and fresh. Their relationship was like wearing a broken watch for show.

When Josie and Phil Weaver decided to separate, they labeled everything in their fridge with masking tape and Sharpie marker: *Phil's orange juice*, *Josie's butter*, etc. When I came over, I'd hunt for things they still hadn't divvied up: crusty sunscreen bottles in the back of the medicine cabinet, stray socks lurking in cobwebs behind the laundry bin. I gathered these things and showed them to Karla, who kissed her parents goodnight at opposite ends of the house before putting herself to bed. "See!" I'd tell her. "There's still a chance!" But Karla lived in the noise of their relationship. Me? Clueless.

Just before Christmas, our girl scout troop took a field trip to the Davenport Theatre to see local performers put on a theatrical adaptation of Charlotte's Web. I'd never seen a play before, but our troop leader kept saying plays were ephemeral, which meant that every live performance could only exist once, because of each night's specific combination of time, place, audience, and current events. No matter how hard a cast tried to replicate their show from the night before, it would never be an exact copy. Karla and I yanked at our eyelids throughout the performance so we wouldn't miss anything.

The actors onstage seemed so tiny from our seats up on the balcony. I tried to imagine them stripping from their costumes and going home at night blown up to the size of regular people. At intermission, I read the playbill cover-to-cover while Karla bought Skittles at the concession stand. It felt weird knowing Wilbur The Pig was just a man named Steve from the next town over who worked as a dentist. When the lights dimmed again, I wasn't sure if I could see the show the same way. Thinking about it too much felt like how it feels when you say a word too many times and it begins sounding like gibberish. Karla got annoyed when she saw me blinking my eyes out of spite.

The ending of Charlotte's Web was happy and sad at once. Charlotte gave birth to a family of beautiful baby spiders, then died in the very same scene, all while her dear friend Wilbur was away.

When Charlotte gave birth, it reminded me of being in the hospital after my aunt had my cousin. I thought about it with my eyes closed while the cast took bows. Sunlight poured into the room—I think my cousin brought it with him—so I wasn't scared, even though my aunt was sprawled out on a cot, looking so weak, linked up to all sorts of machines. The tip of my cousin's nose was faintly blue, like an icicle. The nurses swaddled him real tight so he'd keep warm. I remember one of them saying, "Maybe he's a summer-baby that was accidentally born in the winter." I begged my parents to let me hold him, even though I was just a kid myself. I sat up, attentive, in a chair with my arms outstretched and put on my most mature grin. When they finally put him in my arms, I squirmed, surprised by how heavy he was, in awe of his warmth against my body.

When Charlotte passed away, I didn't have anything to compare it to. My oldest grandparent still came to my softball games and sat in a folding chair on the grass. At one point, the vet thought my friends' dog had cancer, but it ended up being a misdiagnosis.

Phil's orange juice expired. Josie's butter expired.

"Mommy and Daddy grew apart. This happens sometimes with adults. It's only natural," Josie told Karla, all hush-hush, while I waited in the other room. When Karla returned to play, she looked older and more spidery, like she'd aged out of my understanding. Josie pinched my face, wistful. I felt sick and headed home. As I walked back up the street, I kept thinking, *I am so lucky. I want to be lucky forever.* It was a greedy thought and I was ashamed of it.

Divorce affects an orbit of people. At the time, I was on Phil's side—probably because he had just recently taken Karla and I outside to look through his telescope, giving us a crash-course on stars. He had a very specific pocket of knowledge and a certain gravitas that rendered him an expert on the subject. Even then, I liked people who kept passions that couldn't be monetized. It was easier for me, that way, to assume their intentions were pure across-the-board. I felt lukewarm about Josie. At the time, I had a vague distaste for friends' mothers. Spending time with them was like wearing the wrong pair of shoes on a long walk. The mothers in my own extended family felt, in comparison, snug.

There are big chunks of my life I wish I'd written about more in the moment, because trying to recall them by memory is like feeling my way through the darkness to a light-switch. But often, while doing this, I notice new things in hindsight. Perhaps they weren't really there, but they round out the story. They give it hips. They give it toes.

The first summer without Phil was silent: the kind of silence you could hear, laid on thick. Karla and I caught moths in her backyard, our hands dripping wet from the pool. We trapped them under plastic cups and admired their wings. They'd twitch and tremor before becoming still.

HEY, STRANGER

There was an abandoned house at the end of Isabella's street. She told the girls at our lunch-table that she went inside, all alone, and prowled through its dimly-lit halls with the single beam of a flashlight. They were impressed, poking their noses closer and closer as she told the tale, complete with sound effects. I could tell she was lying; she always scratched the side of her leg—a nervous tic—when she did. I could read her well.

The sky was white like clenched teeth. It could've rained, but I knew it wouldn't. We never got that relief, Isabella and I. There was always so much pressure for us to do something big when we were together. We sat with our backs propped up against the front door of the abandoned house. On the porch, a table and chairs waited for a family. We would never sit there. The chairs still held shape—too real. There was even a salt-shaker left from the Last Supper, half-full. A storm blew it onto its side at some point and it stayed like that, defeated by nature.

Isabella sifted through a stack of envelopes from the mailbox. When I gave her a look, she said, "Relax. It's mostly junk."

Even though the house had been empty for years, there was still a part of me that wanted to give it privacy. I think Isabella just liked the rush she'd get from snooping. She was bored. 13's a weird age. How were we supposed to experience anything when we could only get as far as we could walk?

We heard voices. Isabella tucked the stack of mail underneath the doormat and we laid flat on our backs. I turned my head toward her and watched her stomach bob as she breathed, all jittery. This wasn't our first time at the house. It'd become *our* spot—the most exciting trouble we could get into. We did what we could to maintain the initial thrill, the energy that ran through us after we'd mustered up the courage to walk onto the porch; as tame as the whole ordeal was, it was more exciting than bouncing aimlessly on her trampoline for hours, which was our only other option, most days. We'd floss through different yards, around pools and behind sheds, every time we went, rather than taking a direct route from Isabella's place, to assure her little brother wouldn't be able to follow us. The house was ours.

The voices we heard were instantly recognizable: Mr. Howard and Mr. Guerrero, two dads in the neighborhood. Howard's sons played hockey—big shots on the varsity team, and Guerrero's daughter was on Isabella's bus. She painted each of her fingernails a different color. The families had German Shepherds: Daisy and Duke, respectively. Daisy was cute, but Duke was aggressive. Mr. Howard and Mr. Guerrero had a habit of cracking open a few beers and hanging out at the lip of the cold-de-sac on Fridays, talking sports and politics. They were the kind of dads who monopolized the grill at neighborhood BBQs. Howard spoke quick, with passion, force. Guerrero sounded like he had rocks in his throat.

Isabella used to think it was annoying—how I observed everything, even boring parents. She'd snicker when I'd pull out a pen and write down a thought on the back of my hand.

I'm often asked, by people like Isabella, how I'm able to keep a journal as a busy college student.

"Simple," I say. "I make the choice to keep one." I build it into a routine that I stick to.

These people will go, "Must be nice having so much free time," a sentiment I find strange, because nobody would respond that way to somebody who mentions they prefer more extroverted activities as a way to unwind.

I digress.

After the men passed, Isabella got up and said, "I wish we could live here," fingering the keyhole on the doorknob. I knew she'd never turn it. She was all-talk. It's like how she'd dare me to play Bloody Mary during sleepovers in her downstairs bathroom, my bare feet cold on the blue tile, her braces in the mirror. We'd never see anything—obviously—but she'd scream anyway.

We were supposed to be twins—Isabella and I. That's how Mr. Howard or Mr. Guerrero knew me: the girl born from Isabella's rib, a subset of her. Isabella thought we'd die for each other; she loved the mayhem of a promise. She once watched a movie where two kids became Blood Brothers and suggested we do it, whining "It's not like I have AIDS," when I declined.

I softly touched the salt-shaker on the table. "Isabella, this is someone else's house."

"Who cares? Imagine if we ran away and stayed here! We could drop out of school and go on adventures every day! There would be no more rules!" She sighed, dreamily. In her version of us, we'd keep bending toward each other until we were fighting for the same air. Once, she texted me this National Geographic article about how sea otters sleep—floating on their backs, holding hands so they don't drift apart in the water. She wrote, "*This is so us!*"

I got sad thinking of her imagining a future all stuck together with mine. It felt like hearing my own voice on a recording—cringeworthy like that.

Isabella's mom, Teresa, kept plastic covers on all the couches in her house, even the one in the family room where Isabella and I would watch *Jersey Shore* and *Degrassi*. Teresa acted like the world would end if someone walked on her carpet with shoes on. Though I am rather clean and organized myself, I never know what to make of a house that doesn't want to be lived-in. It's hard to decide how to behave in a place like that.

Sal was Isabella's dad. Isabella jokingly called him the Pillsbury Doughboy because he was round and pudgy and always in the kitchen. Early in our friendship, there was an incident where Isabella and I were playing hide-and-seek and I left a door open. He freaked out; he didn't let Isabella have friends over for two months. "If I shut a door, it *stays shut*! That's the *rule*," he yelled, pounding his fist against the wall to emphasize certain words.

Isabella wasn't phased, but it caught me off-guard. She pouted her lips and went, "Looks like the Pillsbury Doughboy is having a bad day. Do you need me to tickle your tummy?" It's always strange to observe another family in a mood.

Teresa and Sal didn't act like parents. They'd give Isabella a heaping pile of Christmas presents, but didn't watch her open them. Once in a while, Isabella would text me real late saying, "Can I bike to your place? Things are bad here." Even if I didn't answer, she'd appear at my bedroom window shortly after, rattling her knuckles against it, until I let her in. She'd curl up at the foot of my bed like a toddler who just had a nightmare and I'd think to myself: *Don't be a hero. Please, don't be a hero.*

Isabella tells everyone that fate made us friends, but we met during a school assembly. We were paired together for an activity because we both had last names that began with the same letter. That's it.

✧

Two hands grab my shoulders. “Hey, stranger."

I turn around, and it’s Isabella, behind me in line at a concert with three girls I don’t know. Her face is soft and thin and her hair is dyed red. She'd look foreign if it weren't for her eyes: forever longing.

"Hey," I mumble. We do an old handshake. It’s rusty, but it’s there—muscle-memory—the way you never forget how to swim or ride a bike. “You got your braces off."

“Uh, yeah.” She licks her teeth. “Ages ago.”

COMPLICATED

My first car broke down last winter, the one I drove since I got my license. It wasn't a sudden thing, but an inevitable and slow decay.

In a way, I was glad. For a while, I truly believed that car was haunted. The heat that poured from the vents felt like smog on my face. I'd have to crack the windows if I wanted to breathe correctly. I'd bob my head in-and-out. *Up for air, up for air.*

Isn't it unsettling how objects have memory? As I was saying goodbye to that car, with its bent and bruised seats, I noticed a small dent on the hood. Immediately, I was pulled back in time. The dent was born after my friend Jared's graduation party, on a June night so humid my glasses frosted white. We made a ring around the pool—my friends and I—talking until the space grew sour. I come from the patterns of suburbia: the foolproof congregation of cars in the McDonalds parking lot on Friday nights because there's "nothing better to do," photocopied white smiles engineered by the same orthodontist, the collective memory of elementary school field-days. I'm very much of the belief that nothing good happens after midnight, and nowhere is this as true as it is during high school summers in my little town.

I felt angry that my car remembered this particular dent. That night, someone suggested I was "too complicated." I don't remember exactly how it was said—whether it was a joke, an insult, or part of some well-meaning advice—but I remember my friends nodding, like: *obviously*. I scooted back from the water, pulling a pool-towel around my legs, suddenly chilly.

"What do you mean?" I asked, eyeing each face. They shrugged me off, feeling the accidental weight of the moment and deciding to opt-out.

I feigned a stomach ache, or maybe willed one into existence, and bolted away quick. I hopped into my getaway car and whipped out of the driveway, accidentally nicking Jared's mailbox as I cut clean into the night, hoping to get as far away from my intensity as I could, grimacing as I imagined it still wafting over the pool like a fragrance.

A few months after my car broke down, Lorde released her 2017 ballad, "Liability." It's not an easy listen. The New Zealand-born pop artist refers to herself as "a forest-fire," and "the only love (she) hasn't screwed up." Her voice is hoarse and shaky. It's a come-down song. She rocks back-and-forth in the aftermath of a high, deciding she's too much for everyone she knows— too complicated.

"Liability" is set in the backseat of a taxi that's fleeing a party. Through tears, New York City—where Lorde penned the track—must've looked congested, dripping with light. My mind makes a map when I listen to it: Point A being the party, Point B being Lorde's cab. "Liability" could've easily been set in a bathroom or a coat closet. I've always been drawn to the sound of a party through a closed door; I think it holds the same tension as watching a party shrink in the distance, a tension that's age-old and evergreen: what I want vs. what I *should* want. It's like the tension of having a headache while everyone else is goofing around or of going to sleep while the others are still up.

"I remember when we were writing, something twanged in the back of my brain that was like–*Ooh! This feels like high school*," I heard Lorde cringe in an interview while recounting the track's conception. I'd agree with her. "Liability" has a sense of theatre that's reminiscent of teenhood; it's a bit pompous and certainly over-the-top. It's not uncommon for a piano-ballad to lean into sentimentality, but, in this case, it happens in a way that disarmed me upon first listen. Lorde is transparent and direct, mourning an ex who "made the big mistake of dancing in (her) storm." She later widens the scope of her sadness, flirting with the idea that she might be "a toy that people enjoy 'till all of the tricks don't work anymore, until they are bored of (her)." I was drawn to her entire sophomore album, aptly titled *Melodrama*, which tries to reconcile with this feeling.

Writing about the self means putting your maturation on display. It's loud and deliberate and insistent on attention. It's done in daylight. To write for an audience, one must be proud.

My first encounter with Lorde was as a pop culture figure, rather than an artist. I remember two friends claiming they heard that the pop newcomer was pretending to be much younger than she was as a gimmick to sell her album. I didn't even like her at first. She seemed like the type of person who was always insisting they were Not Like Most Girls. She rolled her eyes like clockwork and garnered headlines ranting about her supposedly shallow peers. She drew attention to the precarity of fame by using an intellectual gaze to study her ascent as it happened, from "roads where the houses don't change" to limelight, money, clout, and role-modeldom. This distant, wordy analysis of adolescence made up 2013's *Pure Heroine*, which earned her a Song of The Year Grammy at only 16 for the critically-acclaimed, unexpected radio-hit "Royals." At the ceremony, she shuffled onstage in a floor-length vampy black gown, letting her male co-writer thank his people first. Lorde was noticeably tight-lipped in person—more enigmatic than pretentious—a trait at-odds with the precocious voice in her written-interviews.

Some time went by, and I realized it had been a while since I heard anything about Lorde. I assumed she was going to be one of those one-hit-wonders. After a quick dive into her social media, I found out that she purposefully retreated from the public eye for four years following *Pure Heroine*'s success. She returned with an album so hotly anticipated that news of its lead single momentarily broke the internet with the same rigor of an Adele or Beyoncé release. Everyone buzzed in hopes of another humdrum suburban symphony—even myself, since the subtle, quiet angst of *Pure Heroine* eventually came to soundtrack a certain era of my life. Instead, Lorde dropped "Green Light," a bouncy song with a shouty chorus. In the music video, she flaps around in a mini-dress and Adidas Superstars, kicking and punching atop a parked car as her driver looks on, confused. Overall, it got mixed reviews, but I loved it. Lorde was intricate, a maze; she couldn't be boxed.

At the 2017 MTV Video Music Awards, wedged between showy vocal performances from the who's-who of Top-40, Lorde came onstage in sweatpants and spent almost 4 minutes dancing along, quite poorly, to "Homemade Dynamite," a lesser-known cut from *Melodrama.* I was watching at home with my mom the night of. We shared a moment of astonishment about 30 seconds-in when we realized her gawky dancing was the extent of the performance. Both of us hurriedly grabbed our phones to see how people on Twitter were reacting. It was almost as if we couldn't bear to look at the TV. We made excuses—*maybe she's sick! Maybe there was a technical difficulty! No way could this have been what she planned!* But Lorde was smiling. I had never seen her smile on stage before; usually, her eyebrows would thread, pensive, and her top lip would quiver against the microphone. She was having fun: alone-in-your-bedroom fun. Unburdened, she looked young and goofy, like a schoolgirl who'd stand on her desk and wiggle around to make classmates laugh, reveling in the noise of other people's glee.

When we speak of 'amateurs,' we rarely mean hobbyists. We think of the unpaid and unskilled. We think of someone normal, a layman, the antithesis of exceptional. But 'amateur' comes from the Latin 'amare,' — 'to love,' and is there anything more special than the process of loving things just because they make you happy? Over the past two years, I've been taking dance classes at my gym. I love standing right up front, extra close to the mirror. I love seeing my body move clumsily. I love noticing how a smile rises to my face, without fail. That smile is a given—reciprocity, like a hug back.

In the comment-section underneath MTV's YouTube upload of Lorde's dance performance, a puzzled 30-something writes, "I have no idea what this is," to which another commenter, whom I imagine smoking a cigarette outside an indie coffee shop in gentrified Williamsburg, answers, "Go to art school."

Days after the VMAs, I heard Lorde on a podcast, speaking about America's bewilderment and unexpected anger over her bold choice. She decided people were simply uncomfortable watching her experience joy, such a private emotion, in public, adding she too believes it's "quite disconcerting." Contrary to a lot of art, Lorde's performance was self-serving. When she jumped into the air with her legs cocked at the knees, she was trying to touch the sky. When she collapsed onto the floor as if from giggling too hard, she was becoming a child again. It didn't matter that people hated it. It didn't matter that they found her pretentious or attention-seeking. She *had* to do that dance. The audience was an afterthought.

When Lorde gets ugly on *Melodrama*, she doesn't apologize. "I'll love you till my breathing stops / I'll love you till you call the cops on me!" she yelps during the chorus of "Writer In The Dark," never taking it back. She "told you this was melodrama." Take it or leave it.

Melodrama's album cover features artwork by Brooklyn-based Sam McKinniss of Lorde in bed, sandwiched between blankets, curls tumbling off her pillow. Her eyes stare straight ahead, brooding as if she'd been up all night thinking. The image is striking; I love it so much, I had a sticker made of it to put on my laptop. To even use a painting is out-of-the-ordinary, but to have the singer posed so asexually under the covers makes nighttime and the bedroom take on an entirely new connotation in the world of pop. It's not as if *Melodrama* is somehow more prude or wholesome than other work for radio—most of the record is set at a house party; it's just internal. Listeners learn very little about Lorde's ex, who catalyzes the entire project. It's rarely *He did this to me!* but rather, *This is how I felt,* especially on "Supercut," where she realizes how much of the past she's nostalgic for is constructed in idealism, or on "Hard Feelings," where she finds out that she can "start letting go of little things 'till (she's) so far away from (him.)"

On Lorde's 20th birthday, she penned an essay to fans, in which she articulated a handful of coming-of-age anxieties with perfect dexterity. When I first read it, I identified with it so intimately that it made me weep. I remember reading it, thinking: *It's not just me; I'm not alone.* Knowing someone understood why I treated birthdays like funerals provided me with such relief. I have grown out of this phase, of being scared of adulthood, but that doesn't mean it wasn't real at some point. During my first listen to *Melodrama*, I felt woozy, as if I'd turned a corner too fast, hungover on it all. Lorde was so close to the microphone, like she was right behind me, like she *was* me.

I'm very interested in the way pop music illuminates our truths, how it can be a way of reading the self. Rookie Magazine's Editor-in-Chief, Tavi Gevinson, a good friend of Lorde's and an inspiration of mine, gave a keynote speech on this topic at the Melbourne Writers Festival in 2013. After listing some of her most low-brow obsessions, which, at the time, ranged from copying Taylor Swift lyrics into her journal to fangirling over the haircuts of boy-band members, she decided that her devotion and relation to these things was more interesting than the things themselves, since pop culture was her "personal religion," her "moral gymnasium." Watching this lecture on YouTube back in 10th grade gave me permission to feverishly and actively consume things I love, even when they might be considered embarrassing or silly or trashy. I think my fandom has taken on new forms as I've become older and more educated. I read concerts as text. I read fashion as text. I read melodies as text. I contextualize these things within my life story, use them to expunge problems I'm having, hold them when I am cold at night. The ethic of pop is one of pleasure, which is as multifaceted as any other emotional response. Pleasure can look like dancing, screaming, crying, laughing, touching, running, or jumping. We congregate around pleasure. It positions us within a group. It gives us a purpose, a place. When we feel pleasure alone, it is holy, transcendent. Who's to say pop isn't art? Why must I jump-through-hoops to defend it? Does anything matter as much as what matters to me? I think it is beautiful that I am an enthusiast when it is so easy to be a critic.

IN LIGHT LIKE THAT

"I can't believe you got your ears pierced as a baby," Chloe said, on our way into the mall. "That's traumatizing."

"How? I don't even remember getting them done, but I've been able to wear earrings my whole life. It's a win-win," I bragged, gesturing toward my silver hoops. The sky fried orange overhead, the color of honey—pulpy mid-July heat.

A Jeep Wrangler jerked out of its parking space and nearly killed me. The driver rolled down his window and I naively expected an apology, only to be met with "Watch where you're going, bitch!" I am, still, often struck by the anger and rage of other people. I know it's usually disguised hurt—poorly expressed, pent-up, and misdirected—so I sympathize, but I can't relate to the way it explodes from them, like soda from a shaken bottle of Coca-Cola. How could they let their hurt garner such pressure? People are so different from one another.

I only saw the crown of the driver's bald head for a second before he ducked back inside. Chloe gave him the finger and he drove off. He had a bumper sticker that said '*4 Doors For More Whores.*'

"Can you believe women will actually sleep with someone like that?" She scowled. "What a dick."

"I bet you 10 bucks they don't."

Chloe smirked and I felt successful: personally responsible for melting her pissed-off expression, or maybe the sun was just doing what it does best, making everyone look a little abstract, fuzzier, and harder to make sense of. Chloe looked like a mirage in light like that. She looked however I wanted her to look, however I needed her to juxtapose me.

The man at the ear-piercing kiosk dabbed rubbing-alcohol on her earlobes, then dotted each with a blue Sharpie marker. She was given a handheld mirror and glanced into it for a half-second before turning to me. "What do you think? Are they even?"

I was overwhelmed by her trust, so I nodded vigorously and coughed out a froggy "Yes!"

The man hovered the silver gun to her head. She grabbed my wrist first, then slid down into my hand like a finale. I felt a sudden, unshakeable urge to tell someone how good she felt.

Before we left, she bought a pair of earrings to wear in time, when she was allowed to switch out the standard gold studs. Back in her room, I watched as she buried them in her sock drawer, deep, at the very bottom, like a secret.

We went to her family's beach house the next weekend and shared a bed; her ankle hooked around mine under the comforter. Our brains touched while we dreamed. I felt the cool metal of her locket against my cheek. In the morning, we crammed into the same bathroom. I hoisted my leg onto the toilet to shave. She rifled through the medicine cabinet for tampons. We poked at each other's birthmarks, fascinated by each other.

Chloe was the type to collect seashells. Down at the shore, she arranged them on her towel by shape, by size, then by color, holding up certain ones for me to see, squinting through her sunglasses.

Her parents took us to a fancy dinner on our last night away. She did my makeup before we left the house, gently ladling my chin while applying my mascara, my lashes fluttering as her thumb ran along my jawline, up to my ear. I could see colors. I could see pinks and purples and yellows and golds. Touch is a vibrant, mysterious language.

Early August, she and I went to a local carnival with these two guys she knew: Charles and Luca. Charles was 6'3 and apparently wore basketball shorts every day of the year, which she kept saying was "so cute," as if trying to convince herself. Luca ran track and loved gaming and worked weekends at his mom's pizzeria. The boys were leaning against the ticket booth when we got there. They were wearing the same sneakers and the same socks, as if they called each other the night before and coordinated outfits from the knee-down. When he saw Chloe, Charles turned to Luca and said, "I swear to God, this girl gets hotter every time I see her." He spent $50 on carnival games, trying to win her a stuffed animal.

Every time he lost, he turned red-in-the-face. I imagined him beating his chest, animalistic. Chloe laughed and laughed and laughed. Every time she opened her mouth, her giggle sat at a higher pitch. I felt dizzy.

Charles talked about Chloe's body a lot: her '*tight ass*' and '*curves.*' He talked about her body as if it didn't move, as if it didn't house anyone. Had he seen her put her hair in a ponytail without a brush or comb—her beauty effortless, without labor, without tools? Had he seen her ride the motorcycle game at the arcade—twisting her torso, her thighs stuck to the plastic? Had he seen her cook—stopping periodically to taste whatever she was making, lapping her tongue at the spoon? Had he seen her pull on her shoes? Had he heard the sound of her heel sliding in—so tender?

The boys left early and we went on the ferris wheel, just the two of us. It felt nice, floating with her. "Charles kissed me earlier," she told me then, dutifully reporting the moment frame-by-frame. She chose her words like a poet, telling the story as if it were delicate, as if it could break.

While we were still far from the ground, she went, "Can I show you what he did?" and I let her.

I laid up all night thinking, *Summertime: what have you done? What's real now?*

"My brother thinks we're so close we could probably

read each other's minds," Chloe rambled the next day, mounting a playground swing. Her smile was gooey and sweet. It was Golden Hour.

"Try me," I said, giving her a push.

"What number am I thinking of?"

"29."

"Oh my god! How did you get that?"

"I'm psychic," I teased, taking a few steps back so her swing wouldn't take me out.

She laughed. "No, for real!"

"Chlo, you always pick 29! Your phone passcode is literally 2929." I got on the swing next to her, watching her pump higher and higher, using her tan knees and calves. I tried to match her pace. She chatted with a similar athleticism, jumping from topic-to-topic, agile. It was hard to keep up with her that day, because I was overthinking my responses so much. I randomly had a fear of saying the wrong thing, crossing the line, misinterpreting what we were. The park reeked of my childhood, so I felt comfortable in a way that beguiled me.

Chloe slowed down her swing and I followed suit. She stood up to adjust her shorts, then sat down on my lap, her back to my heart. I hung on tight, breathing in the scent of her shampoo. I'll always remember this moment; in my head, it's a piece of our mosaic: the most layered piece of art. She cut it short by saying, "So, I have news."

"What is it?"

"Apparently, Luca thinks you're hot."

"So?"

"*So*, maybe you could see if he wants to go to the movies or something."

"We hung out the other night."

"Not alone!"

"What's the difference?"

She tensed her shoulders. I swear I could feel the temperature change. "It doesn't have to be Luca. Maybe Jeremy from English last year, or the guy from the Fro-yo place—the one that always flirts with you! What's his name again? Matt? Mike?"

"Max."

"Max! If you're not into Luca, he'd be perfect."

"We don't know anything about him."

"He goes to Northwestern. He must be smart!"

"I'm sure he is. That doesn't mean I want to go on a date with him."

"How do you know?"

"I just… *know* when I know."

"That makes no sense!"

"Chlo—c'mon. I'm just not interested."

"Forget it. I don't *care!*" she snapped. "I don't care what you do!" We were quiet for a long, long time. I squeezed her waist so hard. I didn't want her to fall off my lap.

She took me to Luca's pizzeria that night. It was around the corner from her house, in a shopping center where all the stores looked the same from the front. There was no music playing inside, just several TVs blaring CNN at the same time, an overwhelming wave of news and noise. Luca was at the register, swiping someone's credit card. His apron was streaked with grease. Chloe went, "How's it going, Luca?"

"You know how it is," he responded, bagging an order of mozzarella sticks and passing it to a kid in a baseball uniform. Chloe waited for me to say something, but I stared at the floor, counting the beige tiles. She rolled her eyes.

At our table, she asked, "What was that?"

"What was *what*?"

"If you want Luca to like you, you need to stop acting so awkward around him!"

"I don't want Luca to like me."

She snorted. "Oh, yeah?"

"I made it pretty clear that he's not my type. Will you drop it?"

"What's your type? You're so picky." She was acting edgy.

"I don't know. Not him. Why are you doing this?"

"Doing what?"

"You're harassing me about dating! You did it earlier too."

"Oh, fuck you! I'm just trying to help. It's not like you

have guys lining down your block."

I felt my eyes grow wet. I wasn't used to her face looking the way it did, not toward me, at least. "I don't need your help, Chloe."

"You'd be surprised." She barked, snarling. "I do everything for you. You're like a little lost puppy, always following me around when I'm talking to a new guy. It's *sad.* Pathetic. Like—grow up! We're not 15 anymore. I basically had to *beg* Luca to come with us to the carnival yesterday because I couldn't bear to watch you embarrass yourself any longer." The way she talked reminded me of what a snowball looks like as it flies down a hill, picking up speed as it picks up weight.

"Stop it." I shook my head and let out a choppy sentence, monotone, like a toy out of a battery. "I'm figuring it out."

She picked at her straw wrapper, manically, nervously. "What?"

"You know what I mean, Chloe. *You know.*" My voice had never been smaller. "Please don't make me say it."

The words sat between us. A newscaster on CNN told of a murder in Brooklyn, a lying congressman, a plane crash. Chloe leaned back in her chair. She looked at me like I was her world. She got soft again. "Whoever you are is who you should be. Do you know that?"

"Do *you*?"

She winced, shutting her eyes, then reached across the table for my hand. We shared an order of pasta. Our forks waltzed in the bowl. I began to wonder what we looked like from the perspective of someone else in the pizzeria.

For a long time, my heart hurt as if it were a fist in my chest. It wasn't her fault and it wasn't mine. Pain is rarely the fault of those involved. Pain is an environment, an ether, an aura. Pain is as natural as the sun.

Please read me generously. I hate the drama of a confession. Not only is this material low-hanging fruit, but it's so void of spark. I only write about Chloe because she helped me see myself differently, truthfully.

When I write, it sounds like I am egging myself on. I have never been as good at endings as I am at middles. All of my writing comes to me uncontrollably. It sprouts from thin air. I write like one would sew or birdwatch or garden; for me, right now, writing is rational, calm, elderly almost. It's my way of sorting things out. I duck inside, write, then rejoin the world, like taking a nap at lunchtime.

I like writing in the same way I hate arguing. The hot intensity of a moment spoils me—makes me less thoughtful, nuanced, and honest.

I try to write like the weather is nice, even when it's not.

At 21, I am becoming more aware of the weather, which is neither good nor bad, but necessary, because awareness leads to acceptance.

Here's the thing: I want a love without ambiguity, white-picket-fence love. I eventually want to have a wife. She'll do sweet things like make bunny-ears when she ties her shoes, crack jokes that don't quite land. I'll feel safe in her motion. She'll remind me to reapply my sunscreen. We'll give names to clouds that look like animals, playing God. We'll live in a tiny house with flowers sprouting from the lawn. I'll be awoken by the sound of a hairdryer or a toaster oven. We'll frame our children's artwork. We'll thank them for going to school, for asking questions, for being themselves. Their tiny shoes will live in a basket by the front door. Everything in our home will have a home.

It'll get comfortable—us as us—existing in relation to one another. Sometimes we'll sit real quiet, reading different books in the same room, feeling thankful for each other's company. We won't put too much pressure on holidays. On New Years Eve, we'll fall asleep at 11. We'll have our nicest date on February 13th, so we don't die of anticipation. We'll get sick on our birthdays. Because we are human, we'll learn to reschedule.

I'll keep photo albums from childhood—her too. We'll acknowledge the ways in which our lives were rich and hearty long before each other. I'll show her Me at age 4, always walking on tip-toes. I'll tell her what my doctor used to say: "*Maybe she'll end up being a ballerina!*" She'll giggle and I'll say "What? You don't think I'm graceful?" and I'll prance across the room with comedically gangly arms until we're both doubled over in fits of laughter.

I want the halls of our house, like veins, to spider from the center—the heart: a kitchen where we'll eat with our elbows on the table, always leaning in.

Of course, our heaven will be overcast. We'll talk everything out, down to our little pains. I'll weep in the bed because I'm so happy. She'll say, "sweet dreams," like a blessing. The air conditioner will purr, lulling us to sleep.

I have become very good at forgiving myself, which, like accepting the weather, is important, though hard. Letting a grudge fade reminds me of the way old women grow out their gray. It is freeing. When I feel too much guilt or too much regret, there is no space for a story. It is, after all, a myth that sad people are the most creative. People succeed *despite* struggle, not *because* of it.

This all came to me one night on the rooftop of my old elementary school—post-Chloe; we drifted eventually, as people do. My friends and I were waiting for the sun to rise, something we often did during summer breaks from college.

Annabelle, Nia, and Derek laid on their backs, belly-up. I dangled my feet off the ledge, particularly fearless because it was dark and I couldn't see the ground. It was Annabelle's idea to climb up there—Annabelle the wild-one, with her curly, listless mane of hair and thrifted denim jackets. I looked over my shoulder at them, wanting to say, "I love you today," instead of "I love you to death," wanting it to mean just as much. Instead of memorializing our world—our slang, our mannerisms—like I usually did, I was trying something new: letting it all disappear, as if there were no middle-ground. The only thing I wanted to remember was that, for four people so different, we all looked the same up on the roof with the night wrapped around us.

I fiddled with my necklace, wrestling the clasp away from the pendant and fixing it back behind my neck, not thinking anything of the gesture. Annabelle chirped, "Make a wish!"

"On my necklace?"

"When the clasp is at your collarbone, it means someone is thinking about you!"

Nia cackled, "That's such bullshit," her green eyes glowing through the dark.

I spun around to see Annabelle sitting up, all excited. "Don't you wish on your eyelashes?" she joked, scraping the apple of Nia's cheek, blowing an imaginary lash into the air. "It's the same thing."

"Hey! You stole my wish!"

"You snooze, you lose," Derek shrugged, running a hand through his shaggy hair.

Annabelle walked over to me and moved the clasp to the front again. "You get another try."

I pawed at the clasp, noticing the abrupt pause in my chest as Annabelle's words resurfaced. *Someone is thinking about you. Someone is thinking about you. Someone is thinking about you.* She was giddy when she said it, but when it reached my ears, it sounded like another round of violence. I wanted to get away from thinking the opposite of love was freedom, but there I was, squeezing the clasp, squeezing all the magic out of it.

A new perspective came to me, as one always does: a worry is not a premonition. Suddenly, I was bombarded by the words of a coworker who recently gave birth: *you're supposed to forget how painful it was so that you won't be afraid to do it again.*

The sun didn't rise the way we thought it would. It peaked out shyly, then awoke the town with a quick pink explosion. Annabelle, Nia, and Derek snapped pictures of the view for Instagram. I took out my phone too. When I opened my camera app, it faced my way, so I lingered a little to watch my image onscreen. My eyes were teary and I looked like a little girl, worth letting off-the-hook. The morning became baby blue.

✧

"What do you think?" Professor Han asks, lifting her chin at a girl who sits in the back of my college creative writing workshop. I'd just passed around 14 copies of a story I'd written the night before and it was my turn to get feedback.

The girl, Valerie, looks at me hard. "I noticed she only writes happy stories."

"Explain."

"Well, look at the greats; look at our class! Everyone writes really depressing stuff. Her stories are different."

"Are they actually happy though? They are certainly underscored with other emotions," Professor Han suggests. "In this one, we see fear, shame, loneliness—"

"But they always end up in a place many of us don't get to."

"Hope."

"Yeah. Hope."

A sign language interpreter sits in on our class because one of the students is hard-of-hearing. I find it difficult to watch anything else besides his choreography, so precise and intricate; it even involves the face, the eyebrows, the expression. The first time he signs "hope" it looks like he is fanning himself. The second time, he looks like a bird, propelling into flight.

Thank you…

Bethany Rudolf and Betty Ann Medeiros for the wonderful cover art.

Trisha Murphy, Gisselle Jimenez, Hannah Sheridan, Amanda Ettere, Liv Jordan, Stephany Solis, Kyle Alderdice, and Kayla Gorelick for the thoughtful and kind promotional blurbs.

Everyone who's helped workshop and edit pieces from this collection, including professors and scholars at Hunter College and SUNY New Paltz.

Mom, for all your love and support.

www.ingramcontent.com/pod-product-compliance
Lightning Source LLC
Chambersburg PA
CBHW051733020826
48982CB00020BA/1275/J

9780692162170